HUTS, HAVENS
and **HIDEAWAYS**

Jo Denbury with text by Ali Watkinson
photography by Chris Tubbs

HUTS, HAVENS
and HIDEAWAYS

RYLAND
PETERS
& SMALL

LONDON NEW YORK

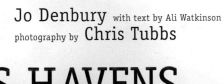

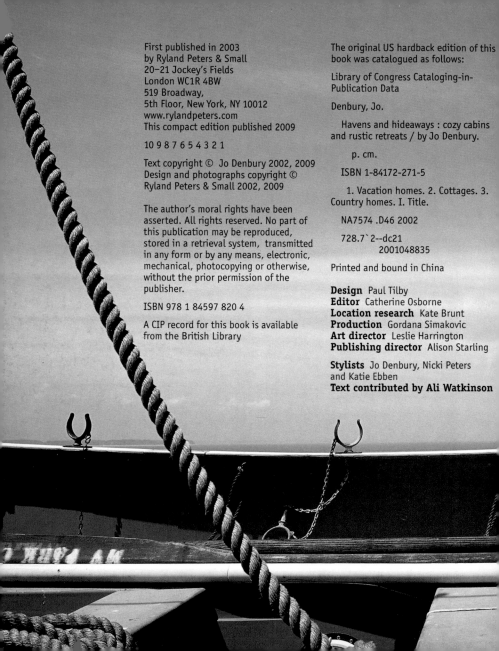

First published in 2003
by Ryland Peters & Small
20–21 Jockey's Fields
London WC1R 4BW
519 Broadway,
5th Floor, New York, NY 10012
www.rylandpeters.com
This compact edition published 2009

10 9 8 7 6 5 4 3 2 1

ISBN 978 1 84597 820 4

A CIP record for this book is available
from the British Library

The original US hardback edition of this
book was catalogued as follows:

Library of Congress Cataloging-in-
Publication Data

Denbury, Jo.

    Havens and hideaways : cozy cabins
and rustic retreats / by Jo Denbury.

    p. cm.

    ISBN 1-84172-271-5

    1. Vacation homes. 2. Cottages. 3.
Country homes. I. Title.

    NA7574 .D46 2002

    728.7`2--dc21
        2001048835

Printed and bound in China

Design Paul Tilby
Editor Catherine Osborne
Location research Kate Brunt
Production Gordana Simakovic
Art director Leslie Harrington
Publishing director Alison Starling

Stylists Jo Denbury, Nicki Peters
and Katie Ebben
Text contributed by Ali Watkinson

CONTENTS

INTRODUCTION

This is a subject that I have been thinking about for a long time, about creating a home that is rooted in our primal instincts. Why? Because I enjoy the rituals of life: making fires, growing vegetables, bathing outdoors, being able to see the stars.

As a child, I lived for a period of time in a house without electricity, and I make no bones about the necessity (and luxury) of mod cons – it is no fun being cold and without power. But what I have noticed is that a lot of us are feeling out of sync with ourselves because we have lost the very essence of what makes us tick. This book is not meant as an answer but more as inspiration. We are living in an era where we increasingly question how we are spending our time. After all, we are born explorers and questers after the unknown, and we spend a lot of time pacing the perimeter of life searching for the answers.

My belief is that it is the very 'high-tech jungle' we have created for ourselves that prevents us from finding these answers. Six thousand years ago man depended on the elements for his life, and today nothing has changed: our bodies are warmed by the sun, our lungs constantly refilled with air, and our vitality depends on taking in water and the fruits of the land. Yet we live

in a time when we feel detached from these necessities. Witness the rise in holidays that take us 'back to basics' – what are we searching for if it isn't to live at one, even for a short period of time, with nature?

The more we embrace technology and material comforts, the more part of us yearns for an altogether simpler existence, one that shrugs off modern-day excesses and returns to a way of life which is part of the natural landscape. There is a simple joy to be found in witnessing the cycle of the seasons, knowing the first frost and, better still, tasting vegetables that have come straight from the earth.

In the future, we will work out what our needs really are. Wage-slavery will be a thing of the past as we realise its futility and the importance of balance in our lives and our homes. Time is the greatest and most valuable commodity of our century, yet we have lost the moment to pause and marvel. This book is about getting back to experiencing the textures of life. This doesn't require huge quantities of money – a recycled railway carriage, an old shack or a boat can all give you space to find time.

Many of the people whose hideaways are featured in these pages talk of a need for solitude, escape, contrast, quiet, emptiness; to be closer to the earth, the weather and the sky and to feel time. This book is intended as an act of celebration for those who have crossed the divide, and as an act of inspiration to those who have yet to go.

water

why
water?

Water is vital to all life: it quenches our thirsts; cleanses our bodies; soothes our minds; and restores our spirits.

The element of water has long been venerated. A century before the Greek philosopher Empedocles directed that the universe was made up of four elements, his fellow thinker, Thale had named water as the ultimate substance; the principal of all things. Its position as a super-element is understandable given its importance to life and its omnipresence. We, and much of the natural world around us, would not exist without water – our bodies are 70 per cent water – and water covers more than two-thirds of the earth's surface.

Luckily for us, water is, without adverse interference, endlessly recyclable. As every schoolchild knows, it rains, rivers form, they flow into the sea, the surface of the sea evaporates, clouds form and, once again, it rains ....

However, as the water conservation expert Peter Warshall eloquently writes, there is more than sustenance in water, there is bounteous pleasure too. 'Water is more than a commodity .... Sloshing around in tanks and ox-bows, swimming pools, and creeks nurtures giggles, sitting by the ocean quiets the soul and steam baths and jacuzzis hold unexplained healing powers of water. In our dreams, reflections, and stories, water as perhaps no other substance gushes with beauty, spirit, grace, and stories of long-term community life.'

healing, sensual
mesmerizing,
cooling, fluid
invigorating
dissolving, reflective
revitalizing
purifying, calming

As each of these hideaways proves, there is an undeniable romance to being by the water, and perhaps even more so when we are actually on the water. One of the havens here is a barge that the owner sails each summer from its city mooring to a rural estuary. By contrast, another is a village dwelling, high above the sea, yet its owner has created an atmosphere where you can almost feel the swell of the sea and half expect to see Tangiers harbour coming into view.

textures, colours, patinas
by the water

ocean, wedgwood
peacock blue
midnight, sky
delft, thistle
slate, cobalt
sapphire, cornflower
indigo, sand
powder blue, dusty
marshmallow
smooth, slippery
chalky, ivory

Water has a surprising number of forms – think of all th words we need to describe them: 'river', 'pool', 'waterfall 'trickle', 'snowflake', 'ocean', 'cloud', 'glacier' are just a few – and it appears in as many colours.

This endlessly varying character and palette may inspire poets, but it is only with the benefit of science that we can explain why frozen water should be white, and why one sea seems blue and another green. The sea commonly looks blue because wate molecules absorb red light and scatter blue light back to our eyes. Areas of the ocean that reflect blue light from the sky wil look bluer than areas that reflect white light from clouds. Yet either chlorophyll from microscopic plants or the reflection of yellow light from sand in shallow water can tinge the sea green Where water droplets or ice crystals are present they scatter light of all colours, sending white light to our eyes.

Whether a frozen pond or a limpid pool, the foam on the sur or droplets in the air, the texture of water is cooling and refreshing, shiny and wet, sensuously satiny. Its texture is also found in the pebbles worn smooth by the ocean and driftwood carved into fantastical abstract shapes; it is damp mossy banks beside a stream, sharp wet rocks underfoot, and the patina lef by salty air beating against our dwellings.

decorate your space with
water in mind

Just as water is cooling and soothing to the touch,
using it as inspiration for the decoration of our homes
can create a similar effect for our eyes and our minds.

The colours of water – white, myriad shades of blue and bluey-
green and silvery metallics – are shades that suggest tranquillity
and space. People are often afraid of these shades, believing
they can make a room seem cold. But think of how deliciously
inviting a still pool of water or a calm sea looks on a scorching
day – hold that colour in your mind's eye – and be inspired to
choose a singing shade that enhances and plays with the light.
Nothing could be cheerier or more redolent of summer.

Blue and white is a classic combination; think of the sky and
clouds and the white spray on energetic waves. It is a squeaky
clean, resolutely nautical style. For a modern update, pair blue
with smooth, silvery metallics. Or be inspired by the textures
and colours of shells and pebbles on the beach and age-worn
stones along riverbanks, to match blue with tactile grey, ecru,
beige and sandy fabrics and accessories – rough linens, hemps
and seagrass matting, for instance – for a more forgiving, less
pristine look.

Alternatively, let blue take a back seat and just use it as an
accent colour in your scheme. See how it clamours for attention,
bringing structure to an otherwise neutral background, just as
the smallest patch of sea glimpsed from miles inland catches
our eye.

'Blue and green should not be seen' – so goes the old saying
– but think of where those two shades overlap and use shades of
turquoise, from deep greeny-blue through to palest aquamarine,
to conjure up memories of oceans stormy and deep or shallow
and tropical.

ISLAND
SHELTER

Why, if we have a fundamental need for personal space, do we deny ourselves the opportunity to escape the city for good? It seems that just as a sauna and plunge pool wouldn't be as refreshingly invigorating or intensely soothing without the other for contrast, a haven could not be such without a completely contrasting existence to escape from.

We may struggle against the challenges of 'real life' but most of us would be lost without them. As the anthropologist Desmond Morris says, 'the city, despite all its faults, acts as a giant stimulus-centre where our great inventiveness can flourish and develop.' A jet-setting, New York ceramicist, the owner of this island retreat was seeking 'a mellow, happy getaway; a place for my partner to write, me to make pottery, and our Norfolk terrier – Liberace – to gambol; somewhere quite different from the insanity of New York.'

'We chose this area because it is only a short ferry crossing from Long Island, yet once you're on the boat you feel totally remote and cut off from things. The minute I'm on the water I feel like I'm on holiday – it acts like a moat, isolating us from our hectic lives. By the time we arrive on the island we are effectively misanthropic shut-ins – to the extent that we become almost feral, barely even bothering to wash or get dressed! We cook, chill, frolic and take dips on the deserted beach and that's about it.'

While the haven is used as often as possible – usually for

three-day weekends – his lifestyle here is, tellingly, not one that he would be comfortable with on a permanent basis, preferring to be able to chop from this Robinson Crusoe existence to its complete opposite, a well-groomed one in 'happening' New York. 'We would love to spend a month or so on the island – the most we can ever manage is a couple of weeks – but I couldn't live there all year round. There's no culture for one thing and when I say we're "feral" I don't mean that feral!'

While the estate agents describe the house as having 'winter water views', the bay is less than a minute's walk away and it is possible to canoe literally from the doorstep via the creek that runs by the house. 'We're constantly on or by the water, swimming, plopping our kayaks into the creek, or throwing the dog into the bay. The water is a constant, reassuring presence.'

Bought as a one-bedroom, one-bathroom shack with a loft, what originally captivated the owner was the property's sense of openness and airiness. Intriguingly, rumour had it that the original structure was built in 1972 by a Pan Am pilot from

Cedar decking rings the house, forming a gentle link between the pristine interior and the deer-inhabited woods beyond.

A wood stove in the living room creates a dramatic focal point and provides the only source of heat. The owners created the quirky fireplace from found stones and pebbles.

Having explored the potential in geodesic domes and Airstream trailers to provide the extra sleeping space they needed for guests, the owners finally commissioned architects to create an extension. The horizontal windows in the resulting master bedroom were designed to give privacy while allowing an eye-level panorama of the enveloping leaves and branches; a sort of living wallpaper.

kit. Architects were retained to create a simple master bedroom and bathroom extension, 'so that we could have our own haven within the hideaway'.

The new part of the house was designed to maintain the handmade, unpretentious quality of the existing 'A' frame building, which suits the relaxed style of the owners and the working-class island, a very different place to the nearby Hamptons. Simple, natural materials like plywood and stone have been given a low-key, subtle textural role by the uniform paint scheme. The blanket covering of white gloss paint hides a multitude of sins, bringing together a hotchpotch of disparate materials and styles to create a clean and airy atmosphere that is unthreateningly modern. It also provides a blank canvas against which to display more homely, personal elements like the owner's own pottery and a bedspread featuring a giant snail shell which he made especially for the house. It's a look the owner describes as 'modern rustic'. For the architects, who are now regular visitors, 'it is a very grounded, down-to-earth house; somewhere you immediately feel at home', while for the owner the atmosphere is above all happy and childlike'.

AILING

BARGE

ving on a boat gives new meaning to the phrase "high
aintenance"', says the owner of this 26 metre (86 foot)
aditional Thames sailing barge, 'as there is always
mething that needs repairing or painting or greasing.'

it is worth the effort for the joy of a peaceful riverside life.
's so quiet; it's like being in the countryside and friends liken
sits to being on holiday. Sitting on the deck with a beer, the
fect is instantly calming. It's fascinating to live so close to
e natural rhythms of the river and sea.'

The barge was a work-
ing boat until 1970
when it was converted
into a houseboat and
its hold was divided
into several rooms.
When the present
owner acquired it, he
removed the partitions
to reinstate the hold
as one vast loft-like,
wood-lined space. As
wood is an incredibly
efficient insulator, the
boat remains cosy
through the winter,
an effect enhanced by
the warm pinky-red
used for the 'lining'.

R.C.

Unusually, this boat is both a city home and a country retreat, for, unlike most of the surrounding houseboats, it is seaworthy. At the beginning of every summer the owner dismantles the huge mast – so that it can clear the many bridges across the river safely – and takes the barge down the coast to a village on the estuary of the River Medway. Here he moors it for four or five months, staying with friends in London during the week and driving down at weekends for sailing parties.

The boat encourages an outdoor life. Its deck is a cheery place to watch the world go by, reclining in the hammock strung between the mast and the shroud. Barbecues, among the anchor and piles of rope, are a regular feature; and sleeping under the stars on a summer's night is especially soothing. 'What's really nice about living on the barge is that my home is transportable. Sometimes I can be down in the hold in my familiar quarters, and it is only when I come up on deck that I remember my "home" has moved many miles from London to a secluded estuary on the coast.'

protective
tactile
rhythmic
swaying
creaking
flowing
therapeutic

In the bow of the boat is a built-in bunk (opposite) in traditional style. At the other end of the space is a salvaged cast-iron bath. Woods of varying ages add character – the floor, actually the 'ceiling' in sailing lingo, is Douglas fir and the sides are oak and pitch pine.

SUMMER
HOUSE

houghtfully positioned to look out through a natural
reak in the surrounding copse, this elegant summer-
ouse enjoys uninterrupted
ews far out to sea.

here is a magical stillness about
is place that takes you away
om real life. I couldn't
nagine anywhere more perfect,'
eclares the owner with heartfelt
assion.

Inspired to create a haven by a childhood
ve of beach huts, she chose a site on
e boundary of her large, overrun garden.
neltered from behind by an ancient, towering yew tree,
ie wood hut nestles in a wooded glade. Lawn and
owerbeds wrap round three sides while directly in front,
rther emphasizing its connection with water, the owner dug
pond. 'I wanted it to feel as if the summerhouse was floating
bove the water.'

Prompted by the simple dwellings seen on a visit to the
est coast of Scotland – where scarce building materials are
eligiously recycled – the owner sourced reclaimed
aterials from all over the island where she lives.
wanted the summerhouse to blend in completely
ith its surroundings, so I searched through vast piles
f assorted timber to find just what I wanted.
eventually came across old barge boarding from a stone
ouse that was being demolished. The old doors are
rench; they were in a poor state with no glass, but then
came across sheets of beautiful old stained glass in pale
hades of blue, pink, green and yellow, and cut out sections

to be set into the corners of the doors and windows. When the sun shines through the glass, the colours dance on the wall behind.' The roof of the summerhouse is covered with cedar shingles which quickly faded to a warm silvery-grey to blend with the distressed exterior. 'We thought about painting the outside,' says the owner, 'but as the structure took shape it seemed to settle into the landscape and visitors say it looks as though it has been here forever.'

The inside has been painted a soft, sea-washed, turquoise blue that positively vibrates in the generous light and connects

It was important to the owner to position the summerhouse where it would be central to plant life and visiting wildlife. 'We love to stand on the seemingly unsupported verandah leaning out over the pond. There is a deep area for water lilies and a shallow area for marginal aquatics, which need to be restricted so that we do not lose the reflections from the oaks and yew trees nearby. Pond skaters, water beetles, toads and dragonflies quickly discovered and colonized it.'

Above all, a haven must be cosy. Here, reclaimed materials, a comfy old sofa and faded floral fabrics lend an old-fashioned, genteel air suggesting that not only has it been here forever, but that tea will be served any minute.

the summerhouse with the colours of the sea and sky that fill the horizon. There is electricity and water laid on and an old French wood-burning stove provides heat. The double doors were designed to open fully so that it is possible to watch the sun rise directly opposite.

'The light streams in off the sea and you wake incredibly early. Here we're witness to all the changing moods of the sea and the sky, and are surrounded by the sounds of the sea lashing in storms and the early morning birdsong. Our time here definitely heightens our awareness of things like the colours of the seasons and the earthiness of a simple place.'

soft
simple
welcoming
reclaimed
bygone
daydreams
time

MEDITERRANEAN
CALM

Occasionally we need to be alone or, at least, alone with our thoughts. Solitude should be a straightforward state to achieve, but in reality something so simple and natural is often impossible given the demands of our lifestyles.

As psychiatrist Anthony Storr has written, '...the capacity to be alone is necessary if the brain is to function at its best. Human beings easily become alienated from their own deepest needs and feelings. Learning, thinking,

The owner painted the walls herself. 'In decoration I am inspired most by artefacts – their faded colours and their history – like the antique ceramic tiles from Portugal which I have used in a patchwork effect on the stairs and in the kitchen area, and the Turkish carpet which suggested the colours for the living room.'

Bright chalky wall
colours like
cobalt and turquoise
– the owner's
trademark as a
interior decorator –
work well in the
sunny climate of the
Mediterranean.
Restricting their use
to below dado height
and pairing them
with white prevents
the strong colours
from dominating and
making the tiny
space look even
smaller.

innovation, and maintaining contact with one's own inner world are all facilitated by solitude.'

Sentiments with which the Italian owner of this tiny, vibrantly decorated house in Provence would undoubtedly agree. Hers is a haven to be completely alone in while escaping the humid summers of Milan. 'I go there to relax. Without my husband, 96-year-old mother, daughter, dog, cats and clients! I need and like to be by myself from time to time.'

Her days here are spent on the terrace reading, drawing and painting. The only social contact comes from visiting the market of the traditional hill town or, in the evening, sitting in the doorway, chatting to her neighbour.

The owner only required a tiny kitchen in which to prepare simple meals, like salads ('I really don't like to cook!' she confesses). By squeezing this into the corner of the living room, space was freed up on the floor above for a boat-style bedroom and a bathroom overlooking the terrace. The French reclaimed zinc bath was cut in half and shortened to fit the space. 'It's the most comfortable bath I'v ever used,' enthuses the owner, 'it's like an armchair.'

Squeezed, higgledy-piggledy, into the ancient town walls, the house is unusually long and narrow – roughly 7 metres (23 feet) deep by 2.5 metres (8 feet) wide. Inspired by its boat-like proportions the owner decided to decorate the small house like a sea-going craft, furnishing it with Mediterranean treasures.

Most of the things are old or reclaimed and come with a story and a patina of use and wear which sit well in the centuries-old house. Booty includes a carpet from Turkey, lights from Morocco, an Arabian screen above the bed and antique ticking fabric from France. From further afield are Indian fabrics and furniture.

In the main living area, colourful Greek-style mattresses, stacked with bolsters and cushions, have been placed along each side, doubling as sofas and bunk beds – when visitors are allowed – and there is a tiny galley kitchen. The owner's bed on the floor above is set – boat style – into an alcove and acts as her 'very own haven'. At night the gleam from a nearby lighthouse shines in the

open terrace doors and washes across the bedroom ceiling. All that spoils the sailing illusion is the house's lofty elevation, some 400 metres (1300 feet) above the sparkling Côte d'Azur.

It could be said that the owner is a fair-weather sailor, as this is a haven just for the summertime when she spends up to two months here – the weather is continuously sunny and a breeze from the mountains 'ventilates' the house. She is attached to her hideaway, but also pragmatic about the disadvantages of living here full time: 'I like village life, but not the whole year round. In the winter, the winds are very strong and cold and none of the houses are heated.' So that is the time she returns to her city life, fortified by her time of solitude.

'How gracious, how benign, is Solitude.'

William Wordsworth

REMOTE
WATERMILL

While our ancestors, in the main, were only too keen to leave the simple, rural life behind, for us returning to a materially impoverished (but spiritually rich) existence has become something of a luxury.

Witness the paradox inherent in expensive holiday destinations trading on their rudimentary facilities: 'No cars, televisions or phones!' 'The wilderness on the doorstep!' Indeed 'luxury' cabins and huts abound, although the travel operators will never go quite as far as labelling them shacks or hovels.

The inversely proportionate relationship that exists between the paucity of material comforts available in a location and the enjoyment to be found there is particularly pronounced at this

The singing blue paint that has been used inside and out is a traditional colour associated with the wood treatment Bleu Charette, a paste-like by product of the production of woad – once a common dye crop in Europe – which is not only beautiful but a natural insect repellent to boot.

riverside hideaway in France. Although remote and unreservedly 'countrified', for its fashion-designer owner and his friends it is 'Heaven on Earth'.

The owner discovered the watermill and adjacent barn 'in an advanced state of disrepair' by accident. The location in the countryside of south-west France is as far from his home and work life in Paris – both physically and mentally – as he could get yet still be on French soil. Set in a lonely clearing, the buildings are 10 kilometres (6 miles) from the nearest village and several kilometres from any other houses. 'The place is very isolated and it's a big effort to get there. But the remoteness is a very important part of being there. I like the quiet and emptiness and relative silence – living in a city for most of the year I particularly appreciate the silence!'

cobalt
remote
rustic
sociable
simple
informal
understated

Little has changed here since the barn and watermill were erected in the early nineteenth century. The converted mill has been simply furnished. 'I enjoy the fact that the buildings originally had a practical, functional use. That they weren't designed for habitation means I have a lot of freedom to live here the way I want. I like empty spaces around me so the layout is completely open-plan and consequently the views from inside are wide-ranging. I have deliberately not "decorated" the buildings, just put in country furnishings and large pieces of furniture whose simplicity appeals to me.'

Although the watermill hasn't operated in 25 years or more, for eleven months of the year the water still courses under and next to the mill, creating 'a serene rocking impression' and acting as a sort of seasonal and meteorological barometer. 'The river changes from season to season, yet is always a strong presence and a source of calm. In high summer it regularly dries up to little more than a trickle. But being in the south, the weather can change very quickly, the river bed suddenly fills

Natural materials have an affinity and sympathy with each another. Here, roughly hewn stone and timber for the buildings, clay for pottery, wicker for furniture, and paint made from natural pigments, sit comfortably with one another, achieving a timeless grace and 'rightness'.

th the watermill
d the barn which
situated alongside
een here) have been
mply furnished and
corated in
cordance with their
nctional origins.
palette of white,
cy and soft blue
s been used on
e mismatched
oodwork to create
harmonious effect
at steers clear of
oking overly
ntrived.

with water from rain in far-off hills and the garden can flood in no time.'

Ironically, given the lack of neighbours and the distance from civilization, socializing with friends is a very important aspect of life at this haven. 'I have lots of visitors here. Often six or so people at a time, and more for special holidays. Everyone does as they please – playing music, reading, chatting or eating long, lazy lunches. There are books everywhere and big armchairs.'

Surrounded by dense plantings of oak and Judas trees, vines, ferns, roses, lilies, clematis and hydrangeas the buildings appear submerged in greenery. 'The house is in a garden, rather than having a garden around the house,' comments the owner, who describes the barn as 'like a boat set in grass'. In the vegetable patch peppers, courgettes/zucchini, tomatoes and herbs are grown for the kitchen. Cooking is an important pastime and the owner loves to work 'with the kitchen doors and windows thrown wide open' so he can continue conversations with friends outside.

Given his connection with the fashion industry, the owner's desire for 'somewhere to be calm and enjoy a timetable-free rhythm', somewhere away from sophistication and formality, is, perhaps, understandable. Three months here every year give him the opportunity to 'do nothing but look, live, cook with produce from the garden and listen to the silence and the sounds of the water running next to the house, the birds, trees and nature all around.'

WHITE-WASHED
BEACH HUT

The poet Carl Sandberg wrote 'Light and air and food and love and some work are enough.' And so they are – the simple pleasures of this beach house perched on the south coast of England satisfy its owners.

Two ladies commissioned this hut to be built in the 1930s as an escape by the sea. Fifty years later, they lent it to the current owners – an artist and a local teacher – who eventually bought it from the ladies, now in their late eighties, a couple of years ago.

'The opportunity to have a second nest was a dream come true. We knew that in this place we would find peace, solitude and a return to a simple life associated with childhood holidays. Even after just a day there I return refreshed and feel as though I have had a proper holiday. Staying there gives us the chance to spend some time together unencumbered by extraneous influences from a busy life, and our time there is very much battery charging. No road passes by and the signals for mobiles/cell phones are often weak because of the weather. The silence is broken only by the sound of waves and the cries of seagulls.'

Being so close to the sea, the exterior of the hut (opposite) requires regular maintenance – an ongoing labour of love – to protect it against the destructive forces of wind and salt. Pebbles are the sea's own handicrafts; tactile and enduringly beautiful. Displayed on ledges (this page) they are ready-made works of art.

As with so many hideaways, the location is everything. The wooden hut stands right on the coastal path, on a large plot of land with 180 degree views of the sea immediately below. The beach is part of a 40 kilometre (25 mile) bank of shingle on the south coast of England. Positioned on low brick pillars, the fierce winds which sometimes batter the coast seem to dissipate underneath. 'The winter and early spring weather can be very dramatic with huge waves and frightening storms. In the summer, conversely, the area enjoys an almost sub-tropical microclimate.'

The area is a magnet for migratory birds. 'Little terns have a well-established summer colony here and last year we had large numbers of clouded yellow butterflies blown over from France. We often see deer in the fields and a large dog fox regularly patrols past at dusk. There are wild flowers in abundance along the shingle banks

Despite the wooden chalet's diminutive size and simplicity, the owners find the want for nothing. I the kitchen, the 1930s dresser (belo has been kept. It maintains the retro look and provides a place for everything from storage to a fold-down surface fe chopping and servir

light
sunshine
fresh air
white paint
utilitarian
compact
powder blue
retro
pillarbox red

lashes of colour – d to help warm and eer the rooms on lil winter days, hen the sea and y are the colour of ato, says the owner, d blues to recall e more summery ues of the sky and a – prevent the all-hite space from oking stark.

including horned poppies, sea cabbage, sea thrift, alliums and viper's bugloss. Our most exciting sight so far was a dolphin just off the coast.'

The rhythm of the sea is a constant presence. 'I am someone who has always needed to be near the sea. It keeps me sane and allows me to live my other life in a more productive way. The light is unlike what you would find inland, and the sunsets are spectacular. We take the same walk every morning and evening and often stop to marvel at the power of the water. Here the sea is dangerously

deep and the weather can change very quickly. When there is no wind and the sea is calm though, it is like a gift, the light turns the sea a bright turquoise and you can swim in safety.'

The hut is south facing, making the most of the sunlight from dawn until dusk. Even in winter months, light pours in. To maintain the feeling of light and to bring simplicity to what is a small space, the hut is painted white throughout. Using white on the walls and ceilings also has the effect of making them recede so the rooms seem

e owners spend up
three months at a
ne at their period
ach hut: 'We try to
t here for most of
e summer, and
ery weekend –
en in winter when
e have to brave the
ements to do so.'

Mod cons extend to
an ancient Baby
Belling cooker, a sitz
bath that 'takes
an age to fill' and oil-
filled radiators. 'Lots
of blankets and thick
duvets keep us warm
in winter.'

larger. Venetian blinds offer an adjustable solution to too much sunlight. The chalet has been kept much as it was in the 1930s. The original furniture remains. Having being designed for the space, it suits the retro style of the chalet and the proportions of the rooms. Shelves of books and the owners' artworks make the place their own. Decorative touches come from natural objects like pebbles, driftwood and shells.

Is this the perfect haven? 'Sometimes we think it might be fun to have all this in a warmer climate but then we wouldn't be as we are, only an hour away from our permanent home, and it is the changing weather conditions and the joy of the unexpected that we love. In truth we are quite besotted with our little hideaway!'

air

why
air?

Of the four elements, air is perhaps the most mysterious. It envelops us and we depend on it for life itself, but we cannot see it. Instead we rely on all our other senses to experience it.

Our sense of smell is a powerful tool in our appreciation of air, and can trigger memories and emotions with remarkable accuracy. We smell warm, summer days in meadow grass and the metallic-like warning of rain to come. Closely linked is taste, as many flavours wouldn't be recognizable without the benefit of smell. For instance, the salty flavour of the air tells us instantly that we are by the seaside.

We hear air, too, in its different strengths and forms, through the whisper of wind through trees and the force of gales rattling windows in their frames. In urban areas we are bombarded by a continuous barrage of noise, and although we are able to sieve out unwanted interference to some extent, its harm is not mitigated. So havens are associated with 'peace and quiet' – but never silence. No matter how far from busy roads we take ourselves, we find nature's background noises   the hum of insects, the roll of waves and the whistle of the wind. They are a comfort and, rather like a lullaby, we can come to depend on them to soothe us into sleep.

'Go outdoors and get some fresh air' is a phrase we all remember from childhood. Experiencing this element is about being outside. Here, we touch the clean, fresh air – as refreshing and invigorating as a cold shower on a humid day. Eating, bathing, showering and sleeping all take on a new dimension with the absence of a roof. One of these havens boasts an outdoor shower on a bridge-like structure that shoots out into the wilderness. At another, the owner swims in a pond dug by himself and drinks 'sun-downers' surrounded by a panoramic view.

soothing, boundless
changing, elusive
transparent
swirling, soft
lofty, blowing
whispering
caressing, breathing
awakening
moving, fresh

textures, colours, patinas
up in the air

Air itself is clear, yet we need only look up at the dome of the sky that stretches from horizon to horizon to witness its myriad colours.

As a rule, air molecules scatter blue light more than any other colour, which is why the sky is generally blue. The shade of blue will vary depending on other factors. Above the ocean, droplets of water suspended in the air scatter white light creating a pale blue sky; the dry air above the desert is purer, resulting in a deep blue sky. By contrast, the blue tone of the sky over our cities fades away in the haze of pollution.

The rainbow is perhaps the most wondrous display of colour in the air. According to Greek mythology, it was the route between heaven and earth taken by Iris, a messenger of the gods. For the Native American Shoshone tribe, it was a giant serpent that rubbed its back against a layer of ice that enclosed the sky. Mankind has always looked to the heavens for divine inspiration. And, just as plants grow up reaching into the sky for sunlight, so we are often drawn to experience the purity of air by climbing up high. Mountain retreats have long been renowned for their therapeutic properties. The owner of a treehouse hideaway describes the feeling he gets up in the treetops as one of escape and of rising above his everyday concerns. Here, among the fresh green growth of the leaves, air feels almost tangible as it brushes past, weightless, never still; always whirling, dancing and invisibly caressing, air provides vital movement and levity. Air's colours are the fresh blues of a clear sky, the young greens of alpine forests; its textures are a cool breeze against our skin, the damp chill of a frosty morning. 'Sharp and crisp' is how the owner of a Scottish hillside hideaway describes this element at its best.

apple, pistachio
chlorophyll
vision, grass
fresh, gauzy
sunshine, radiant
glossy, stippled
seedpods
foliage, emerald
treetops

decorate your space with
air in mind

Fresh air is good for us. A cool wind revitalizes our spirits and refreshes our senses – it blows away the cobwebs.

Houses need fresh air just as we do, so try to keep air on the move. Ceiling fans and air-conditioning units have their place, but natural ventilation is better for us. If possible, a building should be positioned so that a breeze can circulate through all the rooms, as this keeps them fresh and alive, and, of equal importance, cool during warmer months. Note the prevailing direction of the wind throughout the year and plan the position of windows and doors accordingly. Old-fashioned beaded curtains at doorways allow air into a building while maintaining privacy; fine-gauge wire screens do the same job and have the added advantage of keeping insects and other unwelcome intruders out.

Endeavour to remove any barriers to seamless inside–outside living. French windows, stable doors, large picture windows and the like create a visual and physical link between inside and outside spaces that positively encourages outdoor living. Seize every opportunity to eat outside – breakfast, lunch and dinner – it is one of the great pleasures of life. And rediscover the washing line: laundry smells so much better dried in the open air. Hanging sheets outside (aromatic bushes like lavender were traditionally employed as clotheslines) keeps them fresh smelling.

For your interiors, avoid heavy or dark materials and elaborately styled furnishings, which will only weigh a room down. Pale colours and clean lines have the opposite effect. For windows, use ethereal, transparent fabrics like muslin and voile (which are easily washable, too) and discrete blinds to create a fresh, unfussy look that maximizes the light and the feeling of space.

For floors and walls, space-enhancing colours like white and the palest blues and greens suggest airiness. Applying finishes with a sheen will again give an appearance of space by reflecting light. Another way of opening up your home-from-home is to minimize the amount of furniture and clutter you have around you.

SPRUCE-TOP
TREEHOUSE

It's a happy coincidence that the owner of this haven should be a psychotherapist, for the desire to be alone, in a childlike den high up in the treetops raises interesting questions about the human psyche. What might prompt a grown-up to seek refuge in the treetops?

The owner's 'personal-professional view' is very insightful: 'Being up in the air, gives a feeling not just of escape but of "rising above" other concerns,' he says. 'There are childhood connections too: of climbing trees and building swings and dens in the branches, as well as perhaps associations with birds, flying and Peter Pan. It also offers, quite literally, a different perspective on life.'

Built as 'a tranquil place to enjoy nature and the beautiful views and, more practically, to be an extra spare room for guests,' the treehouse is strung between two Norway spruces overlooking a valley. It is close enough to the owner's cottage for electricity to be connected but is so different from life on the ground as to instil the feeling of being, as he says, 'far away from everything'. One advantage of being so near to the cottage is that cooking and washing can be taken care of back at base. However, the climb up has prompted the inclusion of an electric kettle and coffee maker. Most of the owner's leisure time is spent writing in the treehouse, and because it is heated – with an electric radiator – it can be used all year round.

'It really comes into its own in the summer though, when the French windows can be left open. It's ideal to sit about on the

The supporting frame of the treehouse is green oak, attached to the tree using harmless stainless-steel bolts. Cross beams are designed to slide on metal plates so that the house moves with the tree. For the same reason, the windows are mounted in their frames with a flexible rubbery solution. Surprisingly, too much movement has only been a problem on one occasion, when the wind was so strong it caused the treehouse to judder 'rather like turbulence in a plane'.

south-facing deck on lazy days, sunbathing with friends or reading.' The treehouse is positioned so the decking area gets full sun, while the rest remains shaded by branches. 'Being up there overlooking pasture, river and woodland is very calming – particularly if the treehouse is swaying in a gentle breeze. And it adds another dimension to be on the same level as birds when they fly by.'

The treehouse is simply decorated inside, the dominant feature being the tree trunk growing through the structure with its abundant cloak of ivy. White walls emphasize the generous light and contrast with the greenness all around.

Historically, man has felt a need to be part of the cycles of nature. Being in this treehouse puts its owner even closer to the

eyrie
verdant
secret
look-out
camouflaged
elevated
panoramic

changing seasons. 'In summer the valley is in full leaf so everything seems near and lush, rather like a green "sea" when the leaves and branches are swaying in the breeze. In autumn mists shroud the valley floor and the woods are a spectacular mix of russets, golds and reds – very much Keats' "Season of mists and mellow fruitfulness". In winter the landscape recedes and the river can be clearly seen winding through the valley, while spring arrives gently with white blossom on the hawthorn and primroses in the woods.'

Simple materials –
pine decking,
a chipboard floor,
plywood panels – and
a sparsity of creature
comforts lend
a monastic air   the
view is the decoration
– an impression
enhanced by the
Gothic-shaped
windows which are
actually rectangular
panes overlaid with
narrow beading.

BACK TO
BASICS

'Being here is about experiencing the place itself rather than any material comforts; letting the surroundings dominate completely,' says the architect and owner of this barn on a wooded hillside in Vermont

Despite the clever architectural details (and the many examples of classic mid-century furniture) this haven is much more about getting back to basics than designer flourishes. There's no electricity, running water or lavatory for instance – all water

This house in the woods, despite its designer flourishes, is an unsophisticated dwelling at heart. Indeed the owner describes his haven as 'just shelter in the landscape', while his wife sums it up as 'glorified camping'. Yet, despite these deprecatory statements, it is an approach they have been careful to preserve. It would be all to easy to make this get-away-from-it-all experience a mirror image of their home back in the city with all the mod cons we seemingly can't live without. But by resisting such luxuries – even down to plumbed-in conveniences – they are forced to 'rough it'. It is by removing ourselves from our cushioned existences that we are forced to experience the 'cold turkey' of life at its very simplest.

for cooking and washing is pumped by hand from the spring-fed pond. Yet for the owner, who, in his words, 'works like a dog felling trees and chopping firewood' whenever he goes there, the whole experience creates the perfect counterbalance to his loft-living existence in New York City.

Having acquired the 40 hectare (100 acre) site in Vermont several years ago, with the proviso that he wouldn't break it up, the owner unconventionally set about 'inhabiting' the landscape by first creating a pond, then a meadow and then a wood-fired hot tub, before finally starting on the barn or 'hovel' as he calls it, many weekend work parties later. 'Putting it simply, it's just a shelter in the landscape. For me the kick comes from editing that landscape, opening vistas, making the surroundings more airy. This is the way it would have been in the 1800s when this was a hillside farm with more meadow than trees, rather than the other way round as it was when we bought the place.'

Twenty metres (63 feet) long by only 3 metres (10 feet) wide, with a high peaked roof of corrugated metal, the building draws its inspiration from indigenous agricultural buildings, like the covered bridges and tobacco-drying barns of the region.

However, for its ventilation, a 'dog-trot' or open passageway that bisects the building, the architect–owner looked to the South. Thanks to this, even in the height of summer a cool breeze steals through the space. Its full of light, too. The slatted sides of the house appear open to the elements but are actually interleaved with translucent fibreglass, which allows light in and out – to pretty effect at night – while being watertight and bug proof.

Jutting out into the valley on concrete pillars, 425 metres (1400 feet) above sea level, the house was designed to take in the south-facing views of the surrounding mountains. 'We get the best views and the best weather here. Although for me there's no such thing as unpleasant weather. Listening to the rain falling, walking through the snow to get here and heating the place with wood in the winter are all pleasurable aspects of being here – ways to connect back with the rituals of life – just as are physically working hard, carrying water and chopping wood. My time here becomes a sort of meditation through work.' And

Space is a relative concept. Even large rooms can feel cramped if they are badly lit or filled with excess furniture and nicknacks. Positioned on a south-facing hillside to get morning and afternoon sun, the narrow barn is punctuated by a large picture window and ringed by translucent fibreglass slats that, with the sun beaming in, create the effect of being in a giant, airy light box united with the outside.

'Your mind is like a tipi. Leave the entrance flap open so that the fresh air can enter and clear out the smoke of confusion.'

Sioux saying

et there is fun, too, derived from the immediacy of nature and he elements: diving in the pond in summer; skating on it in inter; soaking in the hot tub out of doors; watching the isiting wildlife – deer, bears, wild ducks and turkeys and the ccasional moose – pass by; and shopping for berries, bread, owers and cheese from the organic farm stall miles back along he dirt track.

While his ability to rough it might be unusual, the owner's eed for the haven as a balance to – but not a substitution for his other, urban life is not. Asked could he imagine living ere all year round, he answered succinctly, 'Yes, but no,' efore expanding, 'I'm very comfortable in the country, doing vhat I do there, but I enjoy it more when it is held in contrast o the city side of my life. I like the grit and push of New York ity but I also like the absolute quiet of Vermont.'

The upright stairs (above) – in true settler fashion – lead to a space-saving sleeping platform in the eaves. Great thought has gone into the placement of windows for the best light, views and cooling breezes. The high-level window – matched by one at the opposite end of the barn – ensures effective through-ventilation.

e are so used to the
owded lifestyle of
wns and cities – the
oncrete jungles' –
at seclusion can
me as a shock,
beit a liberating
ie. Here, the
egularity of the
ower supply and the
reat of bears come
and-in-hand with
ie luxury of privacy
id the thrill of
unrestricted freedom
do whatever
ie owners want
henever they want.

MOUNTAIN
LIFE

So high is this escape – 1000 metres (3000 feet) up in the
Catskills – that, in the right weather, the owners can
watch clouds moving through the valley below.

'Being here is very much about experiencing the weather', they
relate. 'The entire south-facing wall of the house is glass, and
looking across the valley – which runs east to west, so we have
the sun all day – towards the hills and mountains opposite,
there is a constantly changing wallpaper of light and sky. We

privacy
open air
freedom
wilderness
seclusion
liberation
outdoors
sky
weather

can spend forever looking at the vastness of the hills.'

A fashion stylist and journalist, both British and living in New York, the couple had been coming to the area for weekends on a regular basis. Exploring one day they came along a dirt road that, after half a mile, led to the concrete foundations of a half-completed chalet deep in the woods. 'The ruins were set on a natural plateau and as we came over the hill the sudden expanse of space below was incredibly exciting. It felt like the south of France with the view and smell of wild thyme that forms a purple carpet all around.'

With the help of an architect, they constructed a shed-like metal-and-wood building that partially used the existing foundations. 'One of the things that really appealed to us about buying this plot was that we weren't eating up a piece of virgin land; the area had already been despoiled and we like the fact that

The hut is bisected by a long, bridge-like structure. At the rear this bridge acts as a gentle pathway leading to the orchard and meadow, but at the front (top left) it is a metaphorical diving board – complete with outdoor shower – into the surrounding wilderness. The owners have deliberately kept furnishings functional – 'when there's so much going on outside you don't need decoration inside.' For the same reason, utilitarian materials like plywood flooring have been used throughout. Consequently, the hut was relatively cheap to build and yet, 'the materials are true to themselves and take a lot of wear and tear.'

the architect's design has incorporated the modern ruin into the house. Being black, the building is a graphic shape that remains static while the surroundings change radically from lush green through the sulphurous shades of autumn to the total white-out of winter. The locals have nicknamed it "the psycho chicken coop".'

Low slung at the back, the hideaway appears settled into the landscape. Taller at the front where the wall of glass is, it appears to open up to the incredible vista, like a wide angled lens capturing the view. Despite this, the couple's time there with their two small children is almost entirely spent outside. 'We do capitalize on our seclusion. There are no visible neighbours and even at night we cannot see the lights of any other properties. We bathe, cook, eat, shower and sleep outside, in effect inverting our loft-living lifestyle in New York so that here the outside becomes the inside. And even in winter we will use the hot tub

Neutral tones create a low-key interior deliberately at odds with the vibrant, ever-changing view from the living room. The fireplace is a vital feature in winter when the power supply often fails, and the well freezes so the owners have to resort to melting snow for water.

ust for the chance to be outdoors when
it would be too cold to stand still
otherwise. It's weird how the privacy
affects you, you end up being quite
reckless and uninhibited!'

Many of us are weighed down by the
clutter of our lives, and it is only by going
outdoors that we free ourselves. This
couple love the outdoors with a passion
'Who isn't a nature lover?' they ask
incredulously. Both brought up in the
countryside, they relish the opportunity
their 10 hectares (23 acres) afford their
own family to create time to think and to
experience the simple freedom to wander
at will, free of crowds, traffic and danger.
Just being able to let the children play
outside in the open air is a luxury. It's a
haven for them as much as it is for us.'

The plywood ceiling
adds warmth and
exaggerates the
feeling of cosiness in
the attic bedroom

(this page). An 'in-
house wood-shop'
supplied most of
the pared-down
furniture, including

the beds and
kitchen. 'Building
things for ourselves
is extra therapy', say
the owners.

RAILWAY
ESCAPE

As this old railway carriage – now at rest on a blustery Scottish hillside – proves, a hideaway need be neither expensive nor far from home. Pragmatically positioned only two minutes' walk from the owner's farmhouse, it is, as he says, 'just far enough to be out of hearing of the telephone'.

Something of an amateur landscape architect, he has brought all four natural elements to bear in the location he chose for the carriage. Sited in a 4 hectare (10 acre) field beneath a typically windswept Scottish mountain, the carriage has magnificent panoramic views across the hillside to the north.

The 1908 passenger carriage (Third Class) was rescued four years ago from a neighbour's garden where it had languished for some 50 years. The wonderfully distressed red paintwork on one side of the carriage has not been retained for its sense of character – 'If it's left like that the wood will only deteriorate!' – but merely indicates a work in progress.

The paint colours chosen for the exterior and interior echo the natural surroundings – the soft greens of the grass and trees and the vivid blues of the pond and sky. Perhaps for the same reason, they seem appropriately Scottish colours such as you might find in a traditional tartan. The roof is coated annually with bitumen. Original fixtures add to the wonderful sense of character and history, and a collection of antique glass bottles plays with the generous light in the sun-room.

The owner has dug a 2 metre- (6 feet-) deep pond, fed by a burn, which he uses for daily swims. And he has planted a 3 hectare (8 acre) native broad-leaf wood nearby with wild cherry, rowan, hazel, birch and elder, and some Scots pine and larch for winter colour.

Although designated the 'summerhouse', the carriage is in use year-round – part cosy nest, part sophisticated 'beach hut' by the pond. In winter, the owner enjoys the effect of cocooning himself in a space smaller than his home. 'When my house is too cold, I often go down to the carriage, light the wood stove and enjoy a good read away from it all.'

This owner has done all the work himself, engendering the feeling of a truly personal space and giving him a sense of 'contributing to and preserving a piece of heritage'. Like many

'Happy the man whose wish and care, A few paternal acres bound, Content to breathe his native air, In his own ground.'

Alexander Pope

of the owners of the hideaways in this book, his relationship with his haven is rather like that of a doting parent with a child. It demonstrates how important it is for us to make room for the things that have meaning to us, and us alone. This doesn't have to be a perfect interior – more often it is a collection of furnishings and accessories cobbled together from the things that we love.

'This is a place for 100 per cent relaxation. There are no negative aspects to it,' he maintains. 'I even enjoy the changing weather, including heavy rain, when I'm in the carriage protected from it all. The lack of luxuries and return to simplicity are very much a positive aspect. I relax as soon as I close the carriage door behind me – the "clunk" sound takes me back 45 years to when I used to travel in similar carriages pulled by steam locomotives. The nostalgia for those days helps me to relax. I think I could very easily live there all year round – it's a nice thought – and perhaps once I've built my privy – American backwoods style – I will. It has all that I need.'

Completely exposed
on a hillside, the
views from the
carriage are far-
ranging; 'There's
masses of sky', is how
the owner puts it.

fire

why
fire?

Fire encompasses heat and light and, through destruction, it begins a process of renewal. It embraces the colours of creativity, joy and passion, and is synonymous with the sun – worshipped, above all else, by ancient civilizations.

We need fire to illuminate our world. Be it the glow of the sun, the flicker of a candle or the slow burn of an electric bulb, the light fire gives out is essential if we are to see. 'Light is so important to us,' writes scientist Peter Ensminger, noting that our eyes have been called 'the great monopolists of our senses'. 'A single glance instantly gives us information about our surroundings that is much more sophisticated than that from our other senses.' Likewise, without light, there would be no colour. The sun's white light contains every colour of the rainbow, and as pigments absorb some of those rays and reflect others, so objects take on the reflected colours.

As well as its light-giving properties, fire is also hot and dry. It bakes the earth in the desert; it burns up the moisture in logs as they crackle and spit in the hearth. Warm spaces and sunny days are synonymous with happy times, and these havens include an Airstream getaway in which the owners find peace under scorching desert skies; there is also a remote Scandinavian retreat that makes the most of every available ray, be it the dwindling sunlight or the glow of candlelight.

We are also compulsively drawn to the warmth and flickering flames of fire, exhibiting the kind of wonder and reverence that our hairier ancestors must have shown when they learned to harness fire's power. In fact, a steadfast faith in the beauty and appeal of a real fire caused one owner here to design his fireplace first and then to build a barn around it. To twist an old homily, 'Home is where the hearth is'.

textures, colours, patinas
from the fire

Fire takes on many forms, and the colour of light emitted indicates the ferociousness with which an object is burning. Red, the colour of cooling lava, is the coldest colour of heat, followed by orange-yellow, the colour of a candle flame, right through to white, the colour of the surface of the sun.

As anyone who has stared into the embers of a fire will know, these shades can coexist, merging and mutating, reflecting the ever-changing presence of carbon and oxygen. Watching fire is to witness transformation.

These are the colours that speed the heart, incite passions and stimulate the brain. Look at how the colour of flames in a hearth merges with the russet tones of logs and the silver of ash. Admire a rosy-fingered dawn and absorb its mix of pale raspberry and frosty blue. Or pick up a pomegranate and note how the reds and yellows merge. The therapeutic use of colour has been popular of late, but the trick to be learned is discovering which colours your body needs.

Fire encompasses extremes – scorching, blinding, burning – yet it is also homely and comforting. It is elusive, magical, uncontainable. Too hot to touch, we can only feel its effects and wonder at its power. We can sense it by the warmth penetrating our bodies sitting next to the fireside, by the heat of the sun on our skin; we can feel hot dry sand beneath our feet, and run our fingers over the cracked earth that has been baked in the desert.

scarlet, emotive
intoxicating
deserts, black
patterned
embers, burned
white hot, blood red
glowing, hot

decorate your space with
fire in mind

Even today, when clean, unobtrusive, under-floor heating is all the rage, a generous fireplace will always form the focus of a room, promising cosiness and refuge. Whatever the style of your decor, don't be afraid to sacrifice space to a real fire. The rewards are multiple, and you will wonder how you could have contemplated life without one.

The colours of fire are intense and advancing – visually, they leap towards you – and used en masse can easily overpower a room, reducing the appearance of space. Highly symbolic, the fiery shades can dramatically alter our moods and feelings: red is the colour of physical drive; pink is calming; orange is the colour of joy and dance; while yellow is intellectually stimulating and optimistic. Think how the room you are decorating will be used and choose your colour palette accordingly. White can also be the colour of fire, but makes a cooling, contrasting counterpoint to the stronger tones, and lifts a space where light is at a premium.

It takes a courageous decorator to use the colours of fire across a whole room scheme, but the effects can be dramatic. Mix several fiery shades together to give interest and to relieve the intensity. Employed as accent colours against a neutral, earthy or cool background, however, these shades add subtle warmth and movement, making us feel cosseted. Warmth in a room also comes from the textures we employ. A deep sheepskin rug, tactile fabrics like chenilles, velvets, luxurious woollens, and minimalist materials such as suede can add to the nesting effect.

Masses of light is top of the modern homeowner's wish list. But too many windows can actually cause problems. Our forebears in climates with cold winters knew not to put windows on the north-facing side of a building and to keep other windows small, so reducing the amount of heat lost. In climates with hot summers windows should also be small, or shaded with overhanging eaves and shutters to keep the interior cool.

DESERT

AIRSTREAM

his quirky haven was an inventive solution to
twofold problem. The owners needed a spare room
o accommodate the regular guests who besieged
heir home to view the San Francisco Bay area.
hey also needed an escape from the '24/7'
ork ethic of Silicon Valley.

Vhen you own your own business and it is
ocated in your house, the only way to escape
om work is to get away,' explain the
usband-and-wife architect team. So, the
ompact 5 metre (16 foot) trailer was
cquired. Bought sight unseen over the
ternet, the 1962 Airstream Bambi, has
dapted well to its double life. Out on the
ad it is an itinerant vacation cottage,
oing anywhere the owners' fancy takes
nem. Parked neatly in the back yard at
ome, it makes an effective self-contained
uest suite.

Having a mobile form of escape gives
he owners a choice of environment.
California spans 24 climate zones,' they
ay, 'and the landscape ranges from very
igh mountains (Mount Witney is 12000
eet above sea level) to Death Valley 240
eet below sea level.' But it is the deserts
hat attract the Airstream's owners. 'The
esert climate is by definition harsh and
he landscape is made even more
ramatic in the winter when the sun is
ow in the sky. Desert winter nights can
e 14 hours long, below freezing, with
inds gusting up to 50 miles per hour.
ut Bambi tempers any weather
onditions.'

The owners have spent, on average,
early a month each year in Bambi,
xploring the many possibilities of living
lose to nature. 'It's beyond the
magination; the mix of elements is
nexhaustible and unpredictable. For us,
here elements clash in nature makes
he best scenery, for instance an oasis in
desert, or a place where mountains
neet the sea.' The Airstream itself is

The owners take
Bambi – the smallest
self-contained model
of Airstream built –
to places which are
too remote to have
lodgings or where
development is not
allowed, such as
in National Parks.
So the fact that
it is entirely self-
supporting – there
is a gas stove,
refrigerator and hot
and cold running
water – is ideal. But
it is a very pared-
down lifestyle, not
unlike camping:
'When you are
independent of the
utility grid you
become acutely
aware of every drop
of water and every
watt of electricity
you use as well as
the waste stream
you produce and
must deal with,'
say the owners.
Its compact size
encourages outdoor
living, as do the
empty acres of desert
at their disposal.

perhaps a perfect example of this clash of extremes, forming a striking contrast between its lustrous, man-made form and the parched landscape of the desert.

The trailer required extensive restoration. Nearly 15 kg (30 lb) in weight of paint was stripped off the aluminium interior and the original heavy enamelled steel stove and sink were replaced with lightweight stainless-steel versions for fuel-saving haulage. Low-wattage light fixtures replaced inefficient steel-and-plastic versions. The owners also replaced a sandwich of vinyl flooring, particleboard and linoleum with two-coloured stripes of a Portuguese cork that is naturally occurring and renewable, and lighter than any other flooring. The stripes help to counteract the narrowness of the

When the owner collected the Airstream 'it had all the aesthetic charm of a roadside men's room'. Today, it gleams inside and out. Cleverly planned, the compact interior adapts from daytime to bedtime with ease – the table folds away and the sofas transform into beds.

space. Where the original fixtures couldn't be bettered, they have been retained. The original 38-year-old propane refrigerator (no CFCs) still works, as does the propane space heater and hot-water heater. And the tiny shower and toilet room remains unchanged – 'the original Italian hand-held shower works better than any shower fixture in our house.'

In the process of restoring the trailer's 'romance of the road' character, the couple have collected aluminium artefacts – cookbook, trash can, ice chest, Ball-B-Q and luggage – dating from the 1930 to 1970s, largely sourced over the internet. Retro fabrics also suit the vehicle's 1960s design and its 'days gone by' atmosphere. But perhaps what most characterizes the decor are the ever-changing arrangements of leaves, sticks, coloured sand and rocks from the owners' latest visit to the desert.

'In the desert, pure air and solitude compensate for want of moisture and fertility.'

Henry David Thoreau

The Airstream's lightweight, aircraft-type construction inspired an 'eco-restoration'. Fittings were assessed both in terms of eco-friendliness and weight (to help with fuel efficiency). For instance, veneered cabinets were rebuilt using aluminium, which is light and avoided the need for petrochemical finishes.

HEARTHSIDE

'I've always been fascinated by fire, so the idea of capturing fire in a vast opening where the focus of the room would be on the flames themselves ... was particularly appealing.'

The fireplace built by the owner-architect of this snug Connecticut retreat, using huge rocks pulled from the surrounding land, is monolithic in scale and design. Lichen still grips the stones and on a winter's night it's not too fanciful to describe the effect as prehistoric and cave-like. 'We burn fires every night from late fall through winter and use candlelight too as it gives a wonderful

The first building on the site was a simple timber-framed house. Later the small house was extended. Outbuildings followed (opposite), then the retreat, all arranged around a 'green' in old New England style, interspersed with oaks and maples. 'I wanted the buildings to be in scale and harmony with the landscape and to have a sense of permanence; to look as though they had always been there,' says the owner.

The retreat is essentially one large room anchored by an expanse of glass at one end and the monumental fireplace at the other. Tucked behind the fire is a bedroom, kept ready for visits by the extended family. The owners also use the space as a retreat from the main house: 'a haven within a haven, we go there to read and relax, and often cook simple suppers in the fireplace.'

glow. Such simple pleasures can be easily overlooked when people get caught up in their complicated worlds.'

Having lived in towns and cities, the owner relishes his new way of life. 'At night I return from the city and like the fact that I can hear nothing of the outside world. It's always a pleasure to come home. This is a wonderfully peaceful place where you're constantly conscious of changes in the weather and the progress of the seasons – each has a distinct character, though the colour of the fall has to make it the greatest season. From October onwards the forest looks as though it is on fire with reds, oranges and yellows. And there's a crispness to the air, a feeling of things changing and getting ready for winter and, of course, we can start stacking wood and laying fires. It's a very special spot; as havens go this isn't bad at all.'

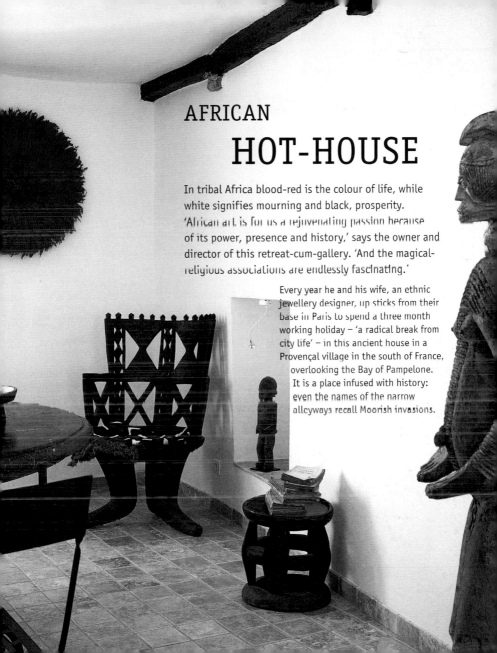

AFRICAN
HOT-HOUSE

In tribal Africa blood-red is the colour of life, while white signifies mourning and black, prosperity. 'African art is for us a rejuvenating passion because of its power, presence and history,' says the owner and director of this retreat-cum-gallery. 'And the magical-religious associations are endlessly fascinating.'

Every year he and his wife, an ethnic jewellery designer, up sticks from their base in Paris to spend a three month working holiday – 'a radical break from city life' – in this ancient house in a Provençal village in the south of France, overlooking the Bay of Pampelone. It is a place infused with history: even the names of the narrow alleyways recall Moorish invasions.

Fiery colours don't need to be used en masse to be effective. Here, isolated, eye-catching splashes of ruby red bring glamour and drama to the otherwise understated rooms. The sculptural, dark-wood furniture – 'the colour of burnt bread', as the owner describes it – is mainly Asian. Although created in a different continent to its final resting place, the hand-made, timeworn quality of the pieces sits well with the simple Provençal cottage and its clay tiles and ancient gnarled beams.

tribal
powerful
symbolic
bold
jewel
bright
contrasting

Living with heat has its own set of problems; here it is solved by thick solid walls and traditional shutters. Employed throughout the Mediterranean countries to let air circulate while keeping out the sun's glare, the shutters keep the house cool, even in summer when the region enjoys relentless sunshine. Inside, the once cramped interior has been opened up and doors done away with to increase the sense of space dramatically. With the shutters thrown open, light courses through, bouncing off uniformly white walls which act as a stark backdrop to the owner's collection of tribal sculptures and textiles and Asian furniture.

In winter, fires are lit in the old fireplace made of traditional, baked clay tiles. 'The weather is mild in the Mediterranean all year round, but we light a fire to create a cosy atmosphere and keep out the damp,' relates the owner, 'We also light lots of brightly coloured scented candles to lift the room and create a relaxing atmosphere.' Outside, the garden is planted with pungent herbs, including thyme, basil and rosemary, and scented plants such as lavender. They release their aroma in the dry heat to fill the air with a relaxing cocktail of aromatherapy.

NORTHERN
LIGHTS

In Sweden, people have had to learn to value the soft beauty and healing effects of natural light, as the days are brutally short through the cold months from mid-autumn to early spring.

The mid-point of the long, dark winter season – the longest night of the year – is marked by the Festival of Light, St Lucia's Day in December, when celebrations centre around the lighting of many candles. Candlelight is an important feature at this converted distillery on a farm in southern Sweden. 'While we do have electric light we rarely use it; instead we burn a large number of candles,' say the owners. 'Artificial light is so strong and cold we prefer the warmth and glow – and the atmosphere of centuries long lost – that candlelight gives.'

The owners are mindful though of the destructive powers of naked flames and open fires. The distillery, being stone, is all that remains of the original period farm buildings which a fire destroyed

st 30 years ago. The outbuildings have nce been rebuilt in the Scandinavian oftwood traditionally used as a building aterial.

The farmstead is some distance from he nearest village, which gives it feeling of isolation that particularly ppealed to the owners. 'For us there is special feeling that comes from living the country and being alone. The eace enhances our closeness to the lements, and we have the knowledge hat nature is always just around the orner for us to enjoy.'

The owners are devotees of 18th- and 9th-century traditional Swedish style – ustavian in particular – and are also ntique dealers. Their antique shop is on he ground floor, while their living space n the first floor benefits from the extra ght that being up in the air affords.

The desire to exploit natural light is ot a purely aesthetic one. Through the inter months, when the sun never rises

Scandinavia, oftwood is ommonly used r building and urniture, so, over he years, paint nishes have been eveloped to protect and to disguise its nsophisticated ppearance. Rich arm colours like eep blue or red re used to merge uildings' exteriors ith the landscape.

airy
reflective
pale
iridescent
gleaming
shadowy
romantic

The romantic, seductive effect of candlelight has become something of a cliché, but – perhaps because we are so used to the all-encompassing reach of electric light – we easily forget what pleasure there is to be had in the patchwork of shadow and glow found in a room lit only by candle- and firelight. We need shadows not just for intimacy but for relaxation and meditation. Where electric light is necessary, restrict its dominance by using task lighting designed specifically for the job in hand.

above the surrounding treetops, spirits can be dimmed along with the sun's rays. The inhabitants of this hideaway recognize this fact and the corresponding need for a regular dose, quite literally, of sunlight to maintain health and happiness. Therefore, as is traditional in Swedish interiors, the layout of the converted distillery is designed and decorated with two conflicting aims in mind: being warm and cosy during the long winters while maximizing every last drop of precious daylight.

Heat-retaining, small windows are offset by pale walls throughout the interior – painted with a traditional soft off-white distemper that gently scatters and reflects the light and complements the light-enhancing whites and grey-blues used on the painted furniture. Internal doors are 'glazed' with fine wire mesh that allows the hazy passage of light between rooms

and at the windows there are simple, traditional rolled blinds, rather than obstructive curtains.

The owners' preference for firelight and candlelight as natural mood lighting immediately creates a warm ambience through the constantly flickering flames and shadows and the associated aromas of beeswax and pinewood that fill the house. The placing of mirrors, sconces and chandeliers combines with the soft light and magnifies it through reflection. It's an old device that originates in earlier centuries when candles were a luxury.

To fuel their passion for firelight, the owners spend the long daylight hours of summer collecting and chopping firewood in the surrounding forests, which they leave to dry ready for the winter months.

Gustavian style is both classical and minimalist. Furnishings are understated and sparsely arranged – a sense of space, freedom of movement and views between rooms are considered essential to creating an airy, light feel. Decoration comes in the form of elegant, light-enhancing accessories such as silver candlesticks and glassware.

earth

why
earth?

We talk of 'Mother Earth', 'going to earth', 'coming down to earth'. Put simply, earth is home, and we have a bond to the ground beneath our feet that cannot be broken.

Yet we take earth for granted. The Vietnamese Buddhist monk Thich Nhat Hanh wrote, 'the real miracle is not to walk either on water or in thin air, but to walk on earth.' Experiencing the element of earth is about experiencing nature. But it is only when we are released from modern pressures, fully immersed in the natural world, that we see its abundant beauty with fresh eyes.

Even confirmed city dwellers have a deep-seated affinity to the earth. You need only think of the treatments on offer at health spas in every metropolis to be reminded of our sensual and spiritual relationship with this element. We smear our bodies in mineral-rich mud; have hot rocks placed on our aching backs; and immerse ourselves in darkened tanks of salt-choked water. It is hardly surprising, then, that so many of us seek a haven where we can reconnect with the earth.

enduring, growth
reassuring
fruitful, home
safety, fertile
bountiful
stability, nurturing
grounding

If you are building your haven from scratch, the siting of the dwelling in the surrounding landscape – its connection with the earth – should be as important, if not more so, than the design of the structure itself. Shelter (the authoritative work on the building of rudimentary huts and hideaways) offers the following inspirational advice. 'Before you decide on a design or materials, you should consider the site: how you will be affected by sun, wind, rain, summer and winter climate, roads, outlook, trees, neighbours, cars, birds ... watch the angle of the sun change throughout the year, learn where the winter storms come from, and figure how to have the morning sun at your breakfast table.'

textures, colours, patinas
in the earth

Earth is the colour and texture of stone, soil, straw, wood, bark, leather and the autumn harvest. Earth is nature's old age; vibrant flowers that are spent and turned to seed heads, green leaves that have fallen and crumbled to humus on the forest floor. Earth encourages us to connect with our environment; it is a tactile element – who hasn't run their fingers through sand, crumbled loamy soil or stroked the knotted whorls on a tree branch?

The colours of earth are reassuring, warm and inviting, the colours of commitment. They immediately make us feel at home, perhaps because they remind us of nature. And what would our homes be like without earth's rich bounty? Without stone for walls and floors, clay for bricks, pottery and tiles, and the different woods for furniture and accessories?

Earth comprises a wide and harmonious palette, one that has been relied on by painters for centuries – think of the mineral pigments of sienna, ochre, umber – a fact recognized by the naming of a mineral-rich region of Death Valley National Park, California, Artist's Palette. And yet many of these colours are the result of compounds formed from a small group of metals – iron, copper and manganese among them. Indeed, iron oxide alone can be red (as in rust), green, pink or yellow.

Earth's many elements have a timeless beauty and character that only improves with age and use. Mix any of these hues and textures together, in any combination, and they will work. They have a sympathy with one another that makes them somehow 'right'.

hazelnut, soil
parchment
bark nutmeg
pelt, stone
pecan, autumn
ochre, peat
cinnamon
clay, putty
sienna, iron
cocoa, umber

decorate your space with
earth in mind

Although essentially grounding, the browns of the earth can magically metamorphose depending on how they are used.

Browns are brought alive by warm, fiery colours like orange and red – think of the colours of a New England autumn. Teamed with white and cream, browns look resolutely chic and modern. Partnered with powder blue or celadon green, they take on a relaxed, sophisticated air. For textural interest, use natural textiles like linen and hemp, and flooring like sisal, rush and seagrass, all of which are incredibly hard-wearing, and whose irregular tones add subtle movement.

Investing in traditional, hand-crafted items – a capacious farmhouse table, deftly woven rush matting – is money well spent. These designs have been tested over centuries, after all, and will be heirlooms for generations to come. So seek out craftspeople who keep traditional skills alive and commission items for your home instead of buying off the shelf. Not only will you have something unique, but you will be reassured that neither the planet nor the maker was exploited in its creation.

Natural colours have a character and subtlety that unites them. Investigate traditional pigments and mix your own paint and dye colours. Take inspiration for shades that sit well together from the natural world. Not only will your house be full of colours that sing out to you – in a way chemical colours can't touch – but you will be saving the environment from unnecessary pollution.

STRAWBALE
HOUSE

There is fun in 'playing house' in any ramshackle or rudimentary dwelling – the smaller the better. This is undoubtedly a throwback to childhood pleasures: camping on the lawn; building lookouts in trees; and constructing wigwams from furniture and blankets!

The owner of this tiny, DIY dwelling was motivated to build her bolthole by 'lack of privacy, stress and a need to escape'. Unusually, it was not city life she was escaping. Sharing her

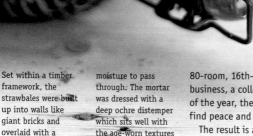

Set within a timber framework, the strawbales were built up into walls like giant bricks and overlaid with a traditional lime mortar. Unlike modern renders lime breathes, allowing moisture to pass through. The mortar was dressed with a deep ochre distemper which sits well with the age-worn textures of the reclaimed door and windows and the soft red of the old clay brick.

80-room, 16th-century manor house with a furniture-making business, a college of residential craftspeople and, for 7 months of the year, the general public, she felt an overriding urge 'to find peace and calm, and to be at one with nature'.

The result is a very intimate and humble abode, completely at odds with her rather grand apartments back in the stately home. 'I wanted to remove myself from "real" life, people, the telephone and from sophistication. I had a yearning for the intimacy of a small space. Time spent in my hideaway is peaceful and productive. I write and garden and daydream –

Despite the 'man-made' environment, there is a feeling that nature envelops the little house entirely. 'The vegetable patch is a tumbling confusion of untidy beauty,' says the owner. 'It's the total antithesis to the formal gardens of the manor house – with rosco, buddleia, clematis left to flower and herbs all intermingled with the many vegetables such as yellow, purple and green beans, unusual lettuces and obscure tomatoes.'

working through problems and gaining a sort of mental "space".'

An accomplished gardener, she felt a need to cement her connection with the rhythms of nature and the earth, and was drawn to create her haven in the derelict Victorian walled kitchen gardens. 'Although within the demesne of the big house, the location is utterly remote in terms of privacy. Most people looking in would have no idea that my hideaway existed. Even on entering the gardens it is not immediately visible; a rose hedge, greenhouse and apple tree hide it from view.'

The strawbale house was built in a corner of the garden against two of the old 4.5 metre- (15 feet-) high brick walls, by her eldest son and a carpenter friend. The bales were built into a timber

The old south-facing brick walls were used by the manor's gardeners for their heat-retaining properties – espaliered fruit trees would have been tied to wires to luxuriate in their warmth. Coupled with the thick straw walls, they keep the space amazingly well insulated. Even in winter the wood-burning stove (opposite) heats the room very quickly, while in summer the deep verandah shades the windows from the direct sunlight and the little house stays pleasantly cool. The makeshift outdoor kitchen (this page) boasts an old Belfast sink, cold running water and an Italian oven with a grill. Water for washing is heated on the stove.

framework – actually old show-jumping poles – and covered with a traditional lime mortar. Contrary to the experience of the Three Little Pigs, strawbale buildings are not easily demolished but are in fact known for their solidity. They are also supremely cheap to build, long lasting and environmentally friendly, because they use renewable, non-toxic, locally available materials and have excellent insulation properties.

'Bird life is wonderful here, varied and very tame. Wrens, fly catchers, robins, blackbirds, finches, nuthatches and owls all visit. There are hedgehogs galore, and wild bees and hornets nest in the garden walls. One feels very close to the elements – yet able to be warm on bitter winter days, or cool on hot summer ones – the ever-changing view of the skies, clouds, sun and moon becomes part of one's immediate consciousness. It would be nice to have far-reaching views, perhaps of the sea, and the opportunity to watch the sunset, but then I wouldn't have the privacy and seclusion.'

ONVERTED
DAIRYHOUSE

nce ancient times, man has had a desire to leave his
ark on the landscape. Yet for a domestic building to
:hieve longevity, it must work both physically with its
wironment and practically for its inhabitants.

tuated alongside a small working farm, nestling in a patchwork
fields, this house is moulded by the gentle slope of the land.
espite the apparent starkness of its design, the relationship

The living room and
eating space focus on
the patchwork of
sheep-filled fields
that stretch across
the valley. In an
effort to be in
sympathy with the
landscape and
existing agricultural

buildings, the house
was built with
untreated materials
like cedar, aluminium
and plywood so that,
chameleon like, they
would weather
quickly and blend
in with the local
limestone.

f the building to the landscape and its inhabitants' experience
f their surroundings has been given great thought. On the
pper level, the old dairy has been converted into three
edrooms and a bathroom. On the lower level, the rickety lean-
o cowshed has been demolished and replaced with a resolutely
odern building, housing the roomy living and eating spaces.
he two levels are connected by a half flight of stairs 'so,' the
rchitects explain, 'there is still the reassuring sensation of
oing up to bed.'

Our sense of touch is what connects us to life. When we feel,
e 'see' with our bodies. Therefore, in creating a place to
scape to, it is important to make it one that adds to your life
n this very real, very tangible way. Here, the space cleverly
ombines the coolness of textured stone underfoot and the
atina of wood to echo the earthiness of the outside.

sympathetic

mellow

weathered

timeless

understated

secluded

natural

seamless

evolving

The space's ease
within its rural
environment is
maintained with
the help of roughly
hewn ceramics,
such as these hand-
thrown pots (above).
Here, even simple
pleasures like
breakfast in bed or
afternoon tea out of
doors seem special.

ECRET
GARDEN

'am not often willing to share my hidden corner of radise,' relates the owner of this rusticated hideaway. fact, I have shown it, with parsimony, to only a few ends and the people closest to me.'

y little garden acts as a retreat when I feel the need to get ay from work and recover some peace of mind. The country ', musty smell of the earth and cold water are, for me, the sence of closeness to nature, whose healing effect unterbalances the hectic, time-structured existence we are rced to live nowadays. Just to cut the grass, look at the wers, sit in the sun on the bench gives me a sense of being away "from the madding crowd". When the time comes to ave, my emotional batteries are recharged and I return full of timism to tasks which previously seemed difficult to tackle.'

The owner has been careful not to alter the atmosphere of the bastidon, so the broken red floor tiles, the patina of the walls and woodwork, and the old tools – now used as decorative objects on the wall – remain, married with rickety chairs and unpretentious fabrics like soft muslin and traditional Provençal prints.

warm
nurturing
earthy
sheltered
rustic
ancient
mysterious
nostalgic

Situated on the outskirts of a medieval Provençal village, the garden and bastidon (a tiny Provençal cottage) may be just minutes away from the owner's home, but the journey there – almost a trip back in time – and the garden's seclusion and simple character contrive to provide all that she requires from her haven. 'From my house in the centre of the village I walk through a medieval stone gate, cross a street and enter a small passage which takes me to the iron gate of the walled gardens surrounding the south side of the town, which are, for the main part, owned by very old ladies who grow vegetables and keep rabbits and chickens there for their families.'

'The longer I stay here the more I feel penetrated by a sensation of being part of a rural past with all that implies. My nostalgia for that past time, "La Vieille

...ance", with which I fell in love as ...child, was what made me leave my ...ative Germany and take French ...ationality. In fact, my attachment to ...e colours, textures and smells of the ...asons, the simplicity of the place and ...e closeness of nature and the past ...ave become an addiction, so much ...that I am reluctant to travel ...sewhere. It is only here that ...truly feel at home.'

SOURCES AND CONTACTS

TEXTILES AND FURNISHINGS

ALMA home
12–14 Geratorex Street
London E1 5NF
+44 (0)20 7377 0762
info@almahome.co.uk
www.almahome.co.uk

Cath Kidston
9a Penzance Place
London W11 4PE
+44 (0)20 7221 4248
mailorder@cathkidston.co.uk
www.cathkidston.co.uk

Celtic Sheepskin
Unit B
Treloggan Industrial Estate
Newquay
Cornwall TR7 2SX
+44 (0)1637 871605
support@celtic-sheepskin.co.uk
www.celtic-sheepskin.co.uk

The Conran Shop
81 Fulham Road
London SW3 6RD
+44 (0)20 7589 7401
for branches
www.conran.co.uk

Eclectics
Pyramid Business Park
Poorhole Lane
Broadstairs
Kent CT10 2PT
+44 (0)1843 608789
www.eclectics.co.uk

Greenfibres
99 High Street
Totnes
Devon TQ9 5PF
+44 (0)845 3303440
mail@greenfibres.com
www.greenfibres.com

Heal's
196 Tottenham Court Road
London W1T 9LD
+44 (0)20 7636 1666 for
branches
www.heals.co.uk

Purves & Purves
+44 (0)20 8893 4000 for
mail order
www.purves.co.uk

Texture
84 Stoke Newington
Church Street
London N16 0AP
+44 (0)20 7241 0990

Whaleys
Harris Court
Great Horton
Bradford BD7 4EQ
+44 (0)1274 576718
info@whaleys-bradford.ltd.uk
www.whaleys-bradford.ltd.uk

FURNITURE

Christopher Tanner
+44 (0)7957 136093
tastesandtextures@hotmail.com

Emily Readett-Bayley
Elmtree House
54 Main Road
Long Bennington
Newark
Nottinghamshire NG23 5DJ
+44 (0)1400 281563
sales@emilyreadettbayley.com
www.emilyreadettbayley.com

Fandango
50 Cross Street
London N1 2BA
+44 (0)20 7226 1777
shop@fandango.uk.com
www.fandangointeriors.co.uk

Habitat
196 Tottenham Court Road
London W1T 7PJ
+44 (0)844 4991122 for
branches
www.habitat.net

Isokon Plus
Turnham Green Terrace Mews
London W4 1QU
+44 (0)20 8994 7032
ply@isokonplus.com
www.isokonplus.com

Julienne Dolphin-Wilding
julienne@dolphinwilding.com
www.dolphinwilding.com

The Mexican Hammock
Company
42 Beauchamp Road
Bristol BS7 8LQ
+44 (0)117 9425353
info@hammocks.co.uk
www.hammocks.co.uk

Places and Spaces
30 Old Town
London SW4 0LB
+44 (0)20 7498 0998
contact@placesandspaces.com
www.placesandspaces.com

Shaker
info@bespokeshaker.com
www.shaker.co.uk

Skandium
86 Marylebone High Street
London W1U 4QS
+44 (0)20 7935 2077
marylebone@skandium.com
www.skandium.com

Twelve
+44 (0)7957 258310
twelvefurniture@yahoo.co.uk
www.twelvelimited.com

FIRES AND STOVES

The Ceramic Stove Company
4 Earl Street
Oxford OX2 0JA
+44 (0)1865 245077
info@ceramicstove.com
www.ceramicstove.com

Diligence
Dart Mills
Old Totnes Road
Buckfastleigh
Devon TQ11 0NF
+44 (0)1364 644790
www.diligenceinternational.com

Twentieth Century Fires
Vesta Works
Greg Street
Reddish
Stockport SK5 7BS
+44 (0161) 4299042
sales@c20fires.co.uk
www.c20fires.co.uk

FLOORING

The Alternative Flooring
Company
Unit 3b, Stephenson Close
East Portway Industrial Estate
Andover
Hampshire SP10 3RU
+44 (0)1264 335111
sales@alternativeflooring.com
www.alternativeflooring.com

Dalsouple
Showground Road
Bridgwater
Somerset TA6 6AJ
+44 (0)1278 727733
info@dalsouple.com
www.dalsouple.com

Fired Earth
Factory shop:
Twyford Mill
Oxford Road
Adderbury
Banbury
Oxfordshire OX17 3SX
+44 (0)1295 814399
+44 (0)1295 812088 for
brochure and showroom details
enquiries@firedearth.com
www.firedearth.co.uk

Forbo-Nairn
PO Box 1
Kirkcaldy
Fife KY1 2SB
+44 (0)800 7312369
www.forbo-flooring.co.uk

LASSCO Flooring
Millstream Road
Bermondsey
London SE1 3PA
+44 (0)20 7394 8061
www.lassco.co.uk

The Original Seagrass Company
Shrewsbury Road
Craven Arms
Shropshire SY7 9NW
+44 (0)845 7666660

Richard Morant
27 Chepstow Corner
Chepstow Place
London W2 4XE
+44 (0)20 7727 2566
richard@richardmorant.com
www.richardmorant.com

sh Matters

e Grange
ange Farm
lesden
dfordshire
4 (0)1234 376419
w.rushmatters.info

INTS AND FINISHES

ro Organic Paints

eltenham Road
sley
roud
oucestershire, GL6 7BX
4 (0)1452 772020
les@auro.co.uk
w.auro.co.uk

eu De Lectoure

cienne Tannerie
nt de l'Ile
700 Lectoure
ance
3 (0)5 62 68 78 30
fo@bleu-de-lectoure.com
w.bleu-de-lectoure.com

rrow & Ball

ddens Estate
mborne
rset BH21 7NL
44 (0)1202 876141
fo@farrow-ball.com
w.farrow-ball.com

tshell Natural Paints

nit 3, Leigham Units
lverton Road
atford Park
xeter
evon EX2 8HY
44 (0)1392 823760
quiries@nutshellpaints.co.uk
w.nutshellpaints.co.uk

tmolen Paint

7 Woodcock Industrial Estate
arminster
iltshire BA12 9DX
44 (0)1985 213960

ose of Jericho

orchester Farm
olywell
r. Evershot
orchester
orset DT2 0LL
44 (0)1935 83676
fo@rose-of-jericho.
demon.co.uk
w.rose-of-jericho.
demon.co.uk

GARDENS

CED

728 London Road
West Thurrock
Grays
Essex RM20 3LU
+44 (0)1708 867237
sales@ced.ltd.uk
www.ced.ltd.uk

English Hurdle

Curload
Stoke St Gregory
Taunton
Somerset TA3 6JD
+44 (0)1823 698418
www.hurdle.co.uk

The Pathway Workshop

Dunnock Way
Blackbird Leys
Oxford OX4 5FX
+44 (0)1865 714111
enquiries@pathway-
   workshop.co.uk
www.pathway-workshop.co.uk

SIMPLE STRUCTURES

Belle Tents

Owls Gate
Davidstow
Camelford
Cornwall PL32 9XY
+44 (0)1840 261556
info@belletents.com
www.belletents.com

Courtyard Designs

Hollywall Farm
Stoke Prior
Leominster
Herefordshire HR6 0NF
+44 (0)1568 760540
enquiries@courtyard
   designs.co.uk
www.courtyarddesigns.co.uk

Haddonstone

The Forge House
East Haddon
Northampton NN6 8DB
+44 (0)1604 770711
www.haddonstone.co.uk

Norwegian Log Chalets

230 London Road
Reading RG6 1AH
+44 (0)118 9669236
www.norwegianlog.co.uk

Osmo UK

Unit 24, Anglo Business Park
Smeaton Close
Aylesbury
Buckinghamshire HP19 8UP
+44 (0)1296 481220
info@osmouk.com
www.osmouk.com

Raj Tent Club

24 Worgan Street
London SE11 5ED
+44 (0)20 7820 0010
nomad@rajtentclub.com
www.rajtentclub.com

Toys for Boys (treehouses)

8 The Manor
Fringford
Bicester
Oxfordshire OX27 8DU
+44 (0)1869 278805
info@treeadventures.co.uk
www.treeadventures.co.uk

Yurt Works

Greyhayes
St Breward
Bodmin
Cornwall PL30 4LP
+44 (0)1208 850670
info@yurtworks.co.uk
www.yurtworks.co.uk

UNUSUAL PROPERTIES
FOR SALE OR RENT

Beach Huts

PO Box 200
Lichfield WS13 6XY
admin@beach-huts.co.uk
www.beach-huts.co.uk

English Heritage

Customer Services Department
PO Box 569
Swindon SN2 2YP
+44 (0)870 3331181
customers@english-
   heritage.org.uk
www.english-heritage.org.uk

The Landmark Trust

Shottesbrooke
Maidenhead
Berkshire SL6 3SW
+44 (0)1628 825920
info@landmarktrust.co.uk
www.landmarktrust.co.uk

The National Trust

Holiday Booking Office
PO Box 536
Melksham
Wiltshire SN12 8SX
+44 (0)870 4584411
(brochure request)
www.nationaltrust.org.uk
www.nationaltrustcottages.co.uk

The Property Organisation

www.property.org.uk/unique

BUILDING ADVICE

The Association
for Environment
Conscious Building

PO Box 32
LLandysul SA44 5ZA
+44 (0)845 4560773
www.aecb.net

Buildstore

Unit 1, Kingsthorne Park
Nettlehill Road
Houstoun Industrial Estate
Livingston EH54 5DB
+44 (0)870 8709991
www.buildstore.co.uk

Ecological Design Association

The British School
Slad Road
Stroud
Gloucestershire GL5 1QW
+44 (0)1453 765575
ecological@design
   association.freeserve.co.uk

SALVO

www.salvoweb.co.uk

FURNITURE AND ACCESSORIES

ABC Carpet & Home

888 Broadway
New York, NY 10003
+1 212-473-3000
www.abchome.com

Anthropologie

Visit the website to find a store near you.
+1 215-568-2114
www.anthropologie.com

The Conran Shop

Bridgemarket
407 East 59th Street
New York, NY 10022
+1 212-755-7249
www.conranusa.com

Crate & Barrel

Flagship location:
646 North Michigan Avenue
Chicago, IL 60611
+1 312-787-5900
www.crateandbarrel.com

IKEA

Flagship location:
1800 East McConnor Parkway
Schaumburg, IL 60173
+1 800-434-IKEA
www.ikea.com

KB Cotton Pillows Inc.

PO Box 57
DeSoto, TX 75123
+1 800-544-3752
www.kbcottonpillows.com

Restoration Hardware

Flagship location:
935 Broadway
New York, NY 10010
+1 212-260-9479
www.restorationhardware.com

Shaker Shops West

5 Inverness Way
Inverness, CA 94937
+1 800-474-2537
www.shakershops.com

Sofa U Love

7545 San Fernando Road
Burbank, CA 91505
+1 818-504-9922
www.sofaulove.com

West Elm

+1 888-922-4119
www.westelm.com
Online Williams-Sonoma store offering many homewares. An onscreen space planner lets you preview how furniture will look in your home.

Williams-Sonoma

Union Square
340 Post Street
San Francisco, CA 94108
+1 415-362-9450
+1 877-812-6235 for your nearest store.
www.williams-sonoma.com

Yield House

Available from:
American Country Home Store
327 Main Street
Ames, IA 50010
+1 800-765-1688
www.americancountry
homestore.com

NATURAL FABRICS

Vreseis Limited

PO Box 69
Guinda, CA 95637
+1 530-796-3007
www.vreseis.com

FLOORING

Hendricksen Natürlich

7120 Keating Avenue
Sebastopol, CA 95472
+1 707-829-3959
www.naturalfloors.net

Image Carpets, Inc.

436 Lavender Drive
Rome, GA 30165
+1 800-722-2504

AIR FILTER SYSTEMS

Aireox Research Corp.

Riverside, CA 92505
+1 951-689-2781
www.aireox.com

Airguard

3807 Bishop Lane
PO Box 32578
Louisville, KY 40218
+1 866-247-4827
www.airguard.com

BUILDING MATERIALS

Building for Health Materials Center

102 Main Street
Carbondale, CO 81623
+1 800-292-4838
www.buildingforhealth.com

Environmental Home Center

4121 1st Avenue South
Seattle, WA 98134
+1 206-315-1974
www.environmental
homecenter.com

ShelterWorks

PO Box 1311
Philomath, OR 97370
+1 541-929-8010
www.faswall.com

Structural Slate Company

222 East Main Street
Pen Argyl, PA 18072
+1 800-67-SLATE
www.structuralslate.com

Terra Green Technologies

1650 Progress Drive
Richmond, IN 47374
+1 765-935-4760
www.terragreenceramics.com

TIMBER

EcoTimber

5215 Central Avenue
Richmond, CA 94804
+1 510-809-8200
www.ecotimber.com

Forest Stewardship Council US

212 Third Avenue North,
Suite 280
Minneapolis, MN 55401
+1 703.438.640
www.fscus.org
Certifies timber from sustainably managed forests.

Goodwin Heart Pine Company

106 SW 109th Place
Micanopy, FL 32667
+1 800-336-3118
www.heartpine.com

Woodworkers Source

18115 North Black Canyon Highway
Phoenix, AZ 85023
+1 800-423-2450
www.woodworkerssource.net

PAINT, FINISHES AND SEALERS

American Formulating & Manufacturing (AFM)

+1 800-239-0321
www.afmsafecoat.com

Auro Organic Paints

Imported by Sinan Company
PO Box 857
Davis, CA 95616
+1 530-753-3104
www.sinanco.com

BioShield Healthy Living Pain

Plaza Entrada
3005 South St. Francis, Suite 2
Santa Fe, NM 87505
+1 505-438-3448
www.bioshieldpaint.com

Janovic/Plaza, Inc.

3025 Thomson Avenue
Long Island City, NY 11101
+1 718-392-3999
www.janovic.com

Zinsser

173 Belmont Drive
Somerset, NJ 08875
+1 732-469-8100
www.zinsser.com

TIMBER FRAME HOMES

Pacific Post & Beam

3450 La Cruz Way, Suite A
Paso Robles, CA 93446
+1 805-434-0166
www.pacificpostbeam.com

Thistlewood Timber Frame Homes

R.R. 6, Thistlewood Road
Markdale, Ontario N0C 1H0
Canada
+1 800-567-3280
www.thistlewood
timberframe.com

ARCHITECTS AND DESIGNERS
WHOSE WORK IS FEATURED IN THIS BOOK

CREDITS

The publisher would like to thank everyone who made the photography for this book possible.

All photographs by Chris Tubbs.

KEY: **a**=above, **b**=below, **c**=centre, **l**=left, **r**=right

Phil Lapworth's treehouse near Bath; **2** Vermont Shack/Ross Anderson, anderson architects; **3** The Stone House in the country in Skane, Sweden; **4–6** Jonathan Adler's and Simon Doonan's house on Shelter Island near New York designed by Schefer Design; **8** Jenny Makepeace's house in Dorset; **16al** A house in Ramatuelle, St. Tropez; **16cl & 16bl** Daniel Jasiak's home near Biarritz; **16bc** Jonathan Adler's and Simon Doonan's house on Shelter Island near New York designed by Schefer Design; **16ar** Mike and Deborah Geary's beach house in Dorset; **16br** Clara Baillie's house on the Isle of Wight; **17** A house in Ramatuelle, St. Tropez; **18–23** Jonathan Adler's and Simon Doonan's house on Shelter Island near New York designed by Schefer Design; **24, 6–27** Vadim Jean's Thames sailing barge in London; **28–33:** Clara Baillie's house on the Isle of Wight; **4–39** A house in Ramatuelle, St. Tropez; **41–47** Daniel Jasiak's home near Biarritz; **48–53** Mike and Deborah Geary's beach house in Dorset; **61al** Vermont Shack/Ross Anderson, anderson architects; **61bl** Daniel Jasiak's home near Biarritz; **61cr** Mike Taitt's railway carriage in Scotland; **61br** Maureen Kelly's house in the Catskills, New York; **62–65** Phil Lapworth's treehouse near Bath; **66–73** Vermont Shack/Ross Anderson, anderson architects; **74–79** Nickerson-Wakefield House in upstate New York/anderson architects; **80–85** Mike Taitt's railway carriage in Scotland; **88 & 93al** Custom Airstream Trailer by Mark J. Marcinik, Greenmeadow Architects; **92 & 93br** The Stone House in the country in Skane, Sweden; **93bl & ar** A cottage in Connecticut designed by Bernard M. Wharton; **93cr** La maison d'un antiquaire en art tribal et d'une créatrice de bijoux à Ramatuelle; **94–99** Custom Airstream Trailer by Mark J. Marcinik, Greenmeadow Architects; **100 & 102–103** A cottage in Connecticut designed by Bernard M. Wharton; **104–107** La maison d'un antiquaire en art tribal et d'une créatrice de bijoux à Ramatuelle; **108–115** The Stone House in the country in Skane, Sweden; **118** Moens Dairyhouse in Dorset owned by Marston Properties Ltd (+44 (0)20 7736 7133); **121br** Jenny Makepeace's house in Dorset; **122l & 123cl** Moens Dairyhouse in Dorset owned by Marston Properties Ltd (+44 (0)20 7736 7133); **123bl** Andrea McGarvie-Munn's garden; **124–129** Jenny Makepeace's house in Dorset; **130–133** Moens Dairyhouse in Dorset owned by Marston Properties Ltd (+44 (0)20 7736 7133); **34–137** Andrea McGarvie-Munn's garden; **144** Vermont Shack/Ross Anderson, anderson architects.

BIBLIOGRAPHY

Writing on Water, David Rosenberg and Marta Ulvaeus. MIT Press, Seattle, 2001.

The Naked Ape, Desmond Morris. Vintage, London, 1994.

Solitude, Anthony Storr. Harper Collins, London, 1989.

ACKNOWLEDGMENTS

I want to say a big thank you to Alison Starling, Sophie Bevan, Gabriella Le Grazie and everyone else at RPS who has worked so hard to produce this book. I am indebted to Chris Tubbs for his beautiful photography and ability to instantly capture the spirit of the book so perfectly. I would also like to thank Ali Watkinson for her excellent and thoughtful writing; Nicki Peters and Katie Ebben for their help in styling for the book; and Ben Kendrick for his suggestions.

A huge thanks to all the people who have let us photograph their private hideaways; without them it wouldn't have happened.

Patience is a virtue that I don't have a lot of but my husband Rupert does. For that I want to thank him and big hugs. Thank you, too, to my sister Fiona for all her ideas and to my mother and father for their inspiration.

Chris Tubbs would like to thank the following for their help, generosity and time: Jo Denbury and all at RPS for letting me work on such a fantastic project. Nicki Peters, Andrea McGarvie-Munn and Chris Brooks for their help. Luis, Steve and Nigel for their support, Dominique for her understanding. A big thank you to those who welcomed us into their wonderful homes.